Lit<

The Ultimate Guide for Understanding Litecoin and What You Need to Know

Copyright 2015 by Elliott Branson - All rights reserved.

This document is geared towards providing exact and reliable information in regards to the topic and issue covered. The publication is sold with the idea that the publisher is not required to render accounting, officially permitted, or otherwise, qualified services. If advice is necessary, legal or professional, a practiced individual in the profession should be ordered.

In no way is it legal to reproduce, duplicate, or transmit any part of this document in either electronic means or in printed format. Recording of this publication is strictly prohibited and any storage of this document is not allowed unless with written permission from the publisher. All rights reserved.

The information provided herein is stated to be truthful and consistent, in that any liability, in terms of inattention or otherwise, by any usage or abuse of any policies, processes, or directions contained within is the solitary and utter responsibility of the recipient reader. Under no circumstances will any legal responsibility or blame be held against the publisher for any reparation, damages, or monetary loss due to the information herein, either directly or indirectly.

The information herein is offered for informational purposes solely, and is universal as so. The presentation of the information is without contract or any type of guarantee assurance.

The trademarks that are used are without any consent, and the publication of the trademark is without permission or backing by the trademark owner. All trademarks and brands within this book are for clarifying purposes only and are the owned by the owners themselves, not affiliated with this document.

Table Of Contents

Introduction

Chapter 1: Litecoin - History and Background

Chapter 2: Litecoin vs. Bitcoin - Pros & Cons

Chapter 3: Understanding Litecoin for Starters

Chapter 4: Getting Started with Litecoin

Chapter 5: More Tips on Litecoin

Chapter 6: What You Need to Watch Out For

Conclusion

Introduction

This short book is for people who are interested in learning more about the Litecoin currency and are not sure where to start or what information to rely on. I made this book in response to the high demand of people wanting to know more about Litecoin and why there is so much hype around it.

The Internet today has a ton of articles and misinformation about Litecoin that confuse people who are interested in learning about this revolutionary crypto-currency and possibly interested in purchasing some Litecoin themselves.

In this book, I am going to give you a short, concise guide for everything you need to know to get started with Litecoin. Understanding the history of this currency, as well as the current innovations that are going on in the Litecoin market, are key to predicting what the future will hold. We will also go over the different functions and options that a person has when it comes to purchasing their own Litecoins and how to use them.

Most importantly, we will go through the pros and cons of using Litecoin so that you can understand the keys before taking the plunge and investing in it yourself. Whether you plan on diversifying from Bitcoin, starting your first crypto-currency with Litecoin, or you just want to know more about why this trend is becoming so popular, it is important to know all the benefits and risks involved.

As a side note, I recommend that you take notes while you are reading this book. This will ensure that you get the most out of the information in here. I want you to feel that you made a purchase that is worth your money and so that you can look over the notes of this book even after you've finished reading it. The notes will help you to pinpoint exactly what you need to implement, and by writing things down, you will be able to recall specifics and how to handle certain situations when they arise.

Lastly, remember that everything in this book has been compiled through research, my own experiences, as well as the experiences of others, so feel free to question what you have read in this book. I encourage you to do your own research on the things that you want to look deeper into. The more you understand about Litecoin, the more educated your decision-making process will be when it comes to purchasing and transacting your own or giving advice to others.

Chapter 1:

Litecoin - History and Background

With the help of fast-advancing online technology, business has taken a revolutionary turn. The Internet is continuously allowing for more thorough invasions of the global business and economic scene. In this process, there have been innovations in the monetary sector, especially with the introduction and subsequent evolution of crypto-currencies – the digital money or medium of exchange used in modern business transactions.

The first universally well-known crypto-currency that was introduced in 2009 was the Bitcoin (BTC). Dozens of different crypto-currencies have followed suit, but it is Litecoin (LTC) that has made it (and still remains) second to Bitcoin in both popularity and user population list. Litecoin is a peer-to-peer digital currency, which was derived from Bitcoin. Using an open-source client on GitHub, the former was introduced on October 7th, 2011 by its maker, MIT alumnus and former Googler, Charles Lee. It was released under the MIT/X11 license.

Litecoin, following its release in 2011, has seen many modifications in the last three years. In November and December of 2013, versions 0.8.5.1 and 0.8.6.1 were released, respectively. Version 0.8.5.1 included updates, bug fixes, and additional security to the Litecoin network. Version 0.8.6.1, which was the latest modification to date, offers a package that includes improved performance and network security, as well as reduced transaction fees by 20 times.

Litecoin is currently the second largest digital currency in terms of market capitalization, trailing only Bitcoin. It reached a market cap of $1 Billion in 2013, and as of January 8th, 2014, its market cap total was $592,061,706.

A proof of Litecoin's growing recognition in the virtual market is its coverage in popular news media outlets such as CNBC, Wall Street Journal and The New York Times. The latter even cited the potential of Litecoin as the Bitcoin successor. In 2013, Litecoin's reputation as a good, if not better, alternative to Bitcoin and its continuous increase in price worth, were well-noted by the paper, The Economist.

Chapter 2:

Litecoin vs. Bitcoin - Pros and Cons

According to Litecoin creator, Charles Lee, Litecoin is a like image of Bitcoin, and as expected, Litecoin's protocol and features are identical to its Bitcoin parent. Litecoin branched out from Bitcoin-Qt client. The main difference between the two crypto-currencies includes the hash algorithm used, their GUI (slightly modified), the number of coins (more), and block generation time (faster).

Despite their similarities, there still exists key differences between Litecoin and Bitcoin (as listed below) that emphasize advantages and disadvantages when choosing one from the other. Further discussions in the following chapters of this book will show that Litecoin is still indispensable in its features and accessibility – the very quality that guarantees a large following among mainstream audiences in the coming years.

Open source protocol

Unlike Bitcoin, Litecoin's creation and transfer can be managed by open source software and procedures. Therefore, the need for a main and central operator is significantly eliminated. This helps Litecoin's case to be a long-term solution in the crypto-currency space.

Speed and accessibility

Litecoin, as stated by its maker, Lee, is more lightweight, hence its name. It provides faster transaction confirmations at an average of 2.5 minutes, compared to Bitcoin's 10-minute usual waiting time, which comprises of the following actions executed consecutively by other users:

(1) Locating of transfers on the Blockchain, Bitcoin's master ledger;

(2) Sending of confirmations and;

(3) Completing of the transaction.

Three confirmations from other users are needed to prove a Bitcoin transaction valid and finally complete it. One confirmation takes 10 minutes; hence the completion of the over-all process takes a total of 30 minutes, much longer compared to Litecoin's 7.5 minute total.

Faster transaction operations of Litecoin means faster block times, which is advantageous in terms of resistance to double spending attacks over a period of time. This occurrence is not always beneficial however, because blocks running faster means increasing block chain length. Consequently, a surge in the number of orphaned blocks becomes highly probable.

Litecoin employs a memory-hard cryptography program known as '***Scrypt***,' which is entirely deviant from Bitcoin's more complex hash program. Scrypt is a sequential, memory-hard program introduced by Colin Percival, which was initially intended to provide more advantage to CPU miners and simultaneously limit the advantage that can be obtained by miners who use GPUs, ASICs and FPGAs.

It was found out later on that GPUs are more efficient in handling Litecoin's Scrypt protocol than were CPUs. Percival also noted Litecoin's poor usage and implementation of the Scrypt protocol. One significant observation was the higher complexity and production cost of FPGAs and ASICs specifically designed for Litecoin mining, compared to Bitcoin's SHA-256.

Despite these setbacks, Scrypt provides efficient and easy mining via usage of consumer-grade hardware, such as those found in CPUs and GPUs generally owned by the common, larger population. For instance, regardless of the fact that CPU mining may not be as trendy and profitable as before, lone CPU miners can still acquire coins if they pool their mines and provide considerable contribution to the network by doing so.

Scrypt is very different from Bitcoin's cryptography, which continuously becomes more complex as Bitcoin grows and expands in its market value. Sophistication and efficiency, which are common qualities of very expensive processor chips, are not a necessity in Litecoin mining. The primary concern of Litecoin is the memory, which can be further improved and expanded by buying faster and better equipment.

Litecoin developers still aim to arrive at an algorithm that can make Litecoin run at the same time with Bitcoin, and on the same hardware employed in mining the latter. The recent surge in the market of specialized ASICs has helped Litecoin to fare well in this goal, although there is still the need to find more efficient solutions to answer the issue of complexity and cost of ASIC utilization.

Audience

In Bitcoin mining, there is a term called "arms race", or a competition to find more mining rigs as fast as possible. There are miners who will try to control the market in order to amass more Bitcoins. This in turn results in overt mining centralization among few miner groups, usually those who possess more expensive and efficient chips as well as technical skills. Litecoin developers tried to counteract this issue by making Litecoin mining profitable enough to accommodate small, conventional miners.

Abundance

The future of Litecoin pictures a skyrocketing projection in the coming years. Just as 21 million Bitcoin units, or more (depending on the market's consistent demand), are expected to be created by 2040, Lee claimed that his Litecoins are projected to almost quadruple the amount of Bitcoins in the same year. Near the end of 2013, Litecoin reached a worth of more than $25, an equivalent to 400% scale up in just a week. Litecoin was declared by its maker to be the "silver to Bitcoin's gold".

Units

Similar to Bitcoin, each Litecoin can be further subdivided into 100,000,000 smaller units. Each unit, in turn, is defined by eight decimal places.

Market Trend

Just like Bitcoin or any other marketable stocks, Litecoin is also subject to unstable, rapid, and drastic price swings. One moment it can amount to a very low price for the day, the next it can balloon up to a very high price.

Chapter 3:

Understanding Litecoin for Starters

Before starting on a chosen hobby or job, it is very important to be knowledgeable of the basics first. Mistakes are inevitable but still, they can be limited and used for improvement. Getting into the Internet currency hype is no different because aside from the fact that Internet technical skills are vital to succeed in this arena, business logic, which can be obtained and enhanced by asking experts' opinions and reading, must not be left behind. Some of the basics that digital greenhorns must include in their notes are listed below:

Language

In order to become a part of the crypto-currency world, beginners must first familiarize themselves with the common words used in a digital *lingua franca*. These include:

Crypto-currency

Digital medium of transaction or exchange, i.e. Internet or virtual money

GPU, FPGA, ASIC, CPU

These are the computer hardware needed

Mining

This is the use of computer hardware, like CPUs and GPUs in Litecoin mining for example, to find enough hash value to create a block and then solve a block, or complete a transaction; this process eventually pays Litecoins

Block

Term used synonymously with a transaction; a solved block means completed transaction, which commonly pays out 50 Litecoins

Blockchain

Series of blocks

Transactions

All transactions, balances, and issuances of Litecoin are handled by the same network that controls Bitcoin. Litecoins are used as a trading unit for fiat currencies and other digital money. Litecoin transactions are fixed and irreversible in order to avoid chargeback issues. Hence, credit cards and other modes of reversible payments are not commonly used when purchasing Litecoins.

Addresses

Addresses where issuance of Litecoin payments occur are based on digital signatures. Digital signatures are composed of strings containing 33 numbers and letters. All signatures will always start with the letter "L".

Confirmations

Every transaction, which is equivalent to a block, is recorded in the Litecoin ledger or Blockchain. A new block attaches itself to the Litecoin Blockchain every 2.5 minutes. A transaction takes a total of 15 minutes to complete, which is equivalent to six solved blocks. Smaller transactions may require less time and blocks to undergo completion.

Wallets

As of January of 2014, there are fewer wallets available for Litecoin, as compared to other crypto-currencies. The most common Wallet employed by Litecoin miners is the Litecoin-Qt, which is an offline wallet. Litecoin-Qt is workable in a wide range of OS, including Windows, Linux, and even Mac. The Litecoin Android wallet was released in mid-January of 2014.

Exchanges

As of today's record, there are a total of 23 market exchanges for Litecoins. The biggest and most well-known among users is the BTC-E. Most of the market exchanges only permit BTC/LTC trading. However, there are three exchanges that allow the trading of Litecoins to US Dollars (USD) and Euros (EUR).

Users' Cafeteria

It is very important for a beginner to learn tips and techniques in regards to Litecoin mining from long-time Litecoin connoisseurs. There are no other sites that can offer a cornucopia of Litecoin information and updates moreso than the official Litecoin forums and on Reddit's /r/litecoin page. The #litecoin IRC channel also provides a new release of updates and software versions.

Chapter 4:

Getting Started with Litecoin

Now that you are familiar with the common terms and basic paraphernalia of Litecoin mining, it is high time for you to board the crypto-currency wagon, if you are still interested. Begin by doing the following procedures:

Establishing Hardware

The first step in building a stable hardware system for Litecoin mining is selecting a good graphics card or GPU. CPU can also be considered, but it would not be quite as fast in mining. For a better and faster system, disregard motherboards, CPU and RAM properties. Motherboards only need to possess enough number of PCI-E slots to accommodate the three GPUs required to build your mining rig. PCI-E may help in a way, by effectively channeling airflow between GPUs and the motherboard, thus preventing any event of overheating.

AMD is better than NVIDIA. AMD Radeon 7950 video cards are a very good hardware choice for Litecoin mining. Due to the popularity, they are often sold out in many stores, but a good substitute is the Radeon R9 280X card. If 280x is still not available, go for 290. The best brands for these Radeon cards include MSI, Gigabyte, and Sapphire.

Next up is the dummy plug for each video card. The dummy plugs ensure that the GPUs will not idle, particularly in the case of using an OS that idles video cards when an active monitor is absent from the system. The idea of dummy plugs is to trick the OS into thinking that an active monitor is connected to the system, which is actually not the case.

Having a USB stick with a memory of 8GB or higher is also essential, particularly if the OS used is Linux. For Windows OS, a hard-drive or any cheap SATA can be used.

Aside from high-performing GPUs, dummy plugs and memory drives, another important factor to consider when designing a system for your rig is the power supply. Running three GPUs will require a tremendous amount of energy. Choose a brand that is highly efficient in providing the most amount of power allowable at a minimum cost, like the Seasonic 860w Platinum PSU.

Lastly, you will need to design a house for your hardware system. Stocking all the said items in a usual PC case is not advisable due to lack of space. It is best to design a larger case for your hardware out of cheap, recyclable materials like plastic crates, in order to skimp even a little on your budget.

Choosing an OS

It doesn't matter if you use Mac, Linux, or Windows for your mining rig system. However, there are specialized setup procedures for each, so be sure to read and follow them carefully to avoid encountering errors along the way.

Acquiring Required Software and other Tools

A. The very first thing to download when you have successfully prepared both the hardware and OS is the Litecoin client and the latest version of Litecoin wallet from Litecoin's official site: www.litecoin.org

After downloading the wallet, run the program and let it sync. Normally, this step takes several hours. After this, a Litecoin address that is unique to the user shall be provided in the Receive tab. Copy the provided address and paste it somewhere, a Notepad for example, because it will be used later on. For security, you may also need to encrypt your wallet with a password or passphrase that you can easily remember.

B. Download the AMD Catalyst 13.1 Software Suite Vista/7 64-bit AMD and AMD APP SDK v2.8 from http://www.techpower...vista-7-64-bit/ and http://developer.amd...-Windows-64.exe., respectively.

Install the AMD Catalyst first, followed by the AMD SDK 2.8. You might need to restart your system after every installation. Never forget this procedure, because doing so will definitely prevent future errors.

C. Now that you have all the drivers installed, you can start learning from your peers. Join in Litecoin official forums or log on to IRC, where you can meet other miners. <u>Joining a pool of miners</u> is advisable to those who are just beginning to learn Litecoin mining schemes, because it requires less work. In a mining pool, the resources of all miners are added up together, and transactions, or blocks, are completed faster. Rewards are also fairly split among miners, so you can still enjoy the fruits of all your labor, even if you did not actually find a block.

To register in a pool, you will be prompted to provide the following information:

Personal Information (Name, Birthday, Age, etc.)

Email

Username and Password

After supplying the aforementioned information, you must enter your PIN and request for an email verification. Log-in to the email address you have provided before, and look for the Welcome Message of the pool where you have just registered. Open the message and get your code.

After acquiring the code, go back to the Account Details page, and supply your Payout Address. Then, create your first worker at My Account, then My Workers. Set a password for your created miner, leave other settings as is, then click Update. For multiple workers or miners, you can use multiple PCs, i.e. one PC for each worker.

D. Download CGMiner or GUIminer mining software from <u>https://bitcointalk....?topic=150331.0</u> to start mining Litecoins. CGminer is considered more advanced than GUIminer, hence experts are expected to use the former and beginners are advised to go for the latter.

However, GUIminer was originally intended for Bitcoin mining. For mining Litecoins, GUIminer Alpha should be the one to work with. Extract the downloaded mining software and run the executable file.

E. For GUIminer: Once the executable file is run, you will be prompted to fill in the required fields. For example, use the Stratum Server stratum+tcp://stratum2.wemineltc.com:3335 or stratum2.wemineltc.com global.wemineltc.com. Do not put HTTPS or tcp:// or port when using the host.

For Port, put 3335. For username field, input the workers name as well as the password that was initially created for it. Always make sure that the stratum box is turned on. Desired settings for GPUs will also be requested. Specific GPU brands and specs will be provided; you just have to select the one you are using from the list of choices.

If you did not find your card on the list, check the Litecoin mining wiki (https://litecoin.inf...ware_comparison) and manually grab the settings for your card.

F. For CGminer: Get the 3.5 version from: http://ck.kolivas.or...ps/cgminer/3.5/, save to desktop and extract. Create a new text document inside the folder. Paste the following command in the first two lines:

setx GPU_MAX_ALLOC_PERCENT 100

setx GPU_USE_SYNC_OBJECTS 1

Followed by:

```
cgminer --scrypt -o stratum+tcp://stratum2.wemineltc.com:3335 -u Tutorial.1 -p 1234 --thread-concurrency 24000 --lookup-gap 0 --gpu-engine 1100 --gpu-memclock 1250 --gpu-powertune 20 -w 256 -I 19 -g 1
```

```
cgminer --scrypt -o stratum+tcp://global.wemineltc.com:3335 -u Tutorial.1 -p 1234 --thread-concurrency 24000 --lookup-gap 0 --gpu-engine 1100 --gpu-memclock 1250 --gpu-powertune 20 -w 256 -I 19 -g 1
```

Click Save As after writing the aforementioned commands, select All Files and name the text file as *My Miner.bat*. The *.bat* extension allows the file to be executed and commands the CGminer to run in Scrypt mode under the specified parameters written in the text document. A list of predefined settings for your card will also be provided. If you are still unable to locate it, manually grab the correct settings in the same wiki site mentioned in the GUIminer section.

G. Begin mining Litecoins!

Chapter 5:

More Tips on Litecoin

Other tips that miners should remember are the following:

1. Buy Litecoins with Bitcoins

Create an account on big exchanges that allow LTC/BTC trades, like Vircurex or BTC-E. Put your Bitcoins in your exchange wallet. Trade your BTC with LTC, and then send your traded Litecoins to your offline Litecoin wallet. Be aware of the rise and fall of Bitcoin prices to ensure that you will get the utmost advantage from the tradeoff. Mcxnow is also a good alternative for buying Litecoins with Bitcoins. Visit: http://mcxnow.com.

If you do not trust exchange media, find a Bitcoin vendor within the country. Personally meeting with a BTC seller can minimize the trouble of wire transfer payments, as well as the possibility of a fly-by-night transaction. However, before purchasing Litecoins with Bitcoins, decide on how many Litecoins you would like to get and calculate how many BTCs you would need. Check the BTC to LTC rate for guidance.

2. Optimize Hardware System Conditions

It is important to do some optimization schemes in your hardware in order to ensure an efficient mining performance, as well as less power consumption costs. One optimization procedure is referred to as "Overclocking of GPUs". This is particularly applicable in CGminers. Increasing clock speeds promises an advantageous mining gain.

Another technique is tweaking the CGminer settings for better system performance and noise management. This procedure greatly helps in reducing power consumption. It also prevents overworking and/or overheating of your GPUs, because standard working operations and conditions are automatically commanded to your system by the CGminer.

3. Analyze the cost and benefit proportion of the Mining Rig System

The success of any business is always determined by more returns over expenditures. The desired result is that the former must always be several notches higher than the latter. If you are just beginning to get on the Litecoin bandwagon, it is highly recommended that you get experts' opinions regarding the best hardware to purchase.

While more expensive hardware and materials guarantee the best performance, there are less expensive ones that can still be (more or less) on par with respect to efficiency in operation, power consumption, and overall mining results. In designing your hardware system for crypto-currency mining, make sure that the ends more than justify the means.

4. Read and Learn More

Crypto-currency businesses require continuous learning because software and program updates and improvements happen every now and then. Such is the norm in the computer world. Read forums, ask questions from experts and buy books to be updated on the newest online trends.

Chapter 6:

What You Need to Watch Out For

In 2013, Bitcoin hit an all-time high with $1,250 price per coin. Starting from a very measly $13 per unit, Bitcoin has had several price swings before arriving to its present value of approximately $800 per unit. Litecoin, being the second biggest crypto-currency next to Bitcoin, fares in the market today in almost the same manner as Bitcoin did a few years back. Litecoins amount to $24 per coin presently, which is a little higher compared to Bitcoin's initial price. However, investors who have been left out during the Bitcoin craze have high hopes for Litecoin in the coming years.

Just as there are positive things to hope for in the crypto-currency world, there are also negatives that people must watch out for as well. One thing to be worried about is online theft.

Thefts in online business can be as dangerous as the crimes we see in real-world business. Sometimes, online crimes can be much worse. The Internet is too broad and even fast for many of us to comprehend. It is not easy to trust it with our personal information, because even names and account numbers from protected bank sites can be stolen, as we've seen with large companies like Bank of America.

Crypto-currency mining is not 100% safe either. That's why Litecoin mining experts and beginners alike must be vigilant and careful when handling transactions and giving out information. As much as possible, avoid online wallets, and be responsible when mining with pools. Keep your Litecoins in your personal and protected Litecoin wallet.

Be extremely wary when buying Litecoins, especially from unaccredited sites. When sending money to a seller or market exchange, it is advisable that you meet the operator in person. When buying Litecoins using Paypal or credit cards, be sure that the transactions are made with accredited media, like VirWox.

Remember, Litecoin and Bitcoin services are not highly monitored yet. There is neither a central bank nor authority that regulates virtual money like physical assets such as gold bars, that can back up crypto-currencies. However, losing digital money is the same as losing real money. You still lose something financially. The worst thing with digital currency is, even if you can view theft cases in the transaction ledger of Blockchains, the culprits have the advantage of anonymity. Hence, frauds and thieves can still operate freely even after scamming other people.

Just remember, practice caution at all times but after you've learned as much as you can and taken the proper precautions, don't become too hesitant to take action. Now is a great opportunity to get into Litecoin!

Conclusion

I hope this short book was able to help you learn more about the basics of Litecoin, the different options you have, and how the future looks for this new currency. Now that you have learned the important factors regarding Litecoin, you can finally decide if you want to take the plunge, or if you can recommend this to your family and friends.

Plus, a little addition to your knowledge doesn't hurt, right? It's good to know about new innovations because it keeps you in the know and up-to-date in a world where every big city has groups dedicated to learning more about crypto-currencies.

Finally, if you learned something from this book please take the time to share your thoughts by sending me a message or even posting a review to Amazon.

Thank you and good luck!

Printed in Great Britain
by Amazon